Helping Children See Jesus

ISBN: 978-1-933206-86-8

Salvation in the South Seas
A Story of Fiji

Published by Scripture Union in England and used by arrangement with them
© 1960 by Patricia St. John
Scripture Union USA: PO Box 987 #1, Valley Forge, PA 19482
CANADA: 1885 Clements Road Unit 226, Pickering ON L1W 3V4

Author: Rose-Mae Carvin
Cover Illustration: Linda McInturff   Illustrator: Frances H. Hertzler
Typesetting and Layout: Morgan Melton, Patricia Pope

© 2018 Bible Visuals International
PO Box 153, Akron, PA 17501-0153
Phone: (717) 859-1131
www.biblevisuals.org

All rights reserved. No part of this publication may be reproduced, stored in a retrieval system or transmitted in any form by any means, electronic, mechanical, photocopy, recording or otherwise, without the prior permission of the publisher, except as provided by USA copyright law.

RELATED ITEMS

To access related items (such as activities, memory verse posters and translated texts) please visit our web store at shop.biblevisuals.org and enter 5520 in the search box on the page.

FREE TEXT DOWNLOAD

To access a FREE printable copy of the teaching text (PDF format) in English or other available languages, enter S5520DL in the search box. Add the item to your cart, and use coupon code XTACSV17 at checkout. Once your order is processed you will receive an email with a link to the free download.

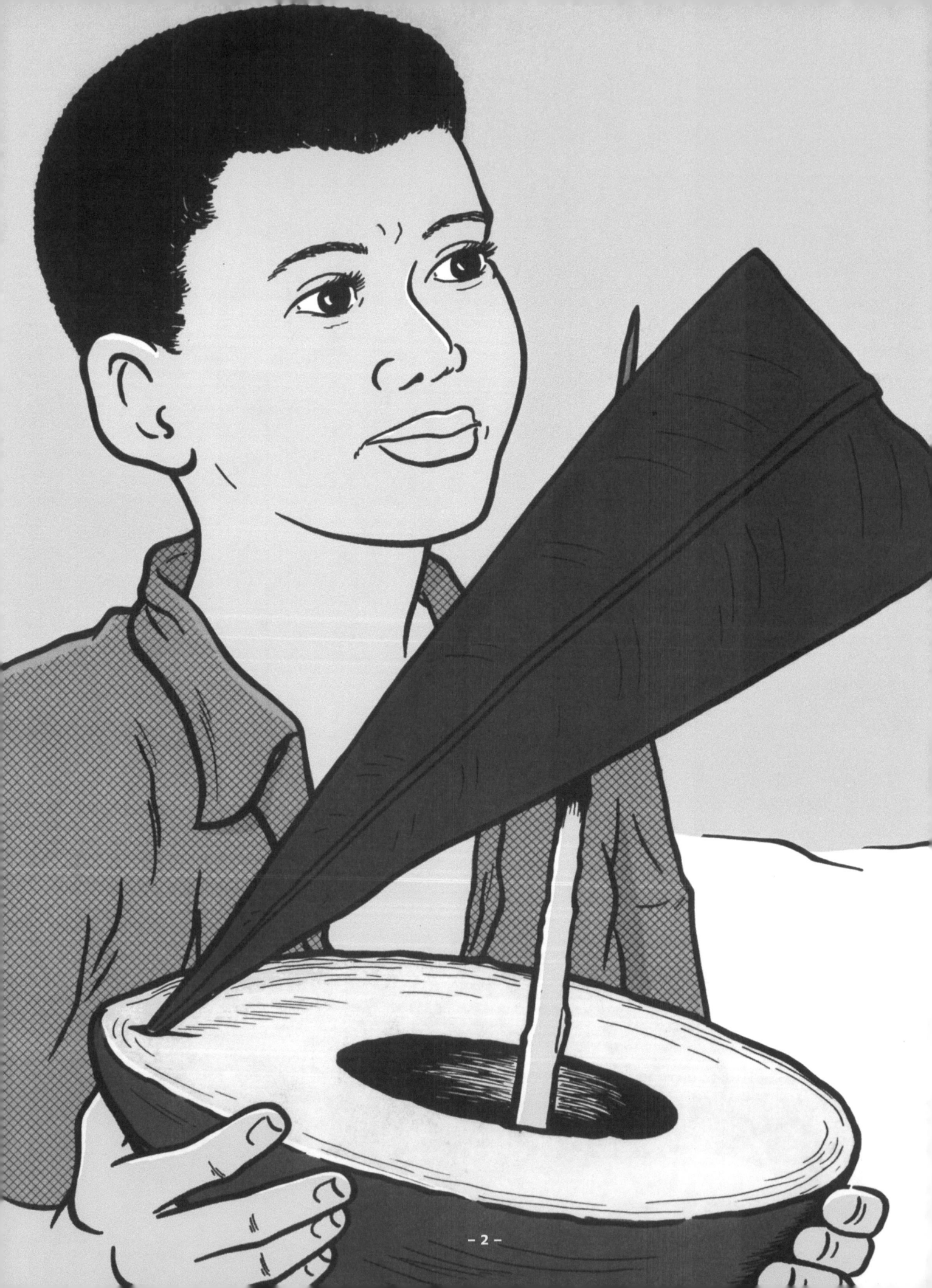

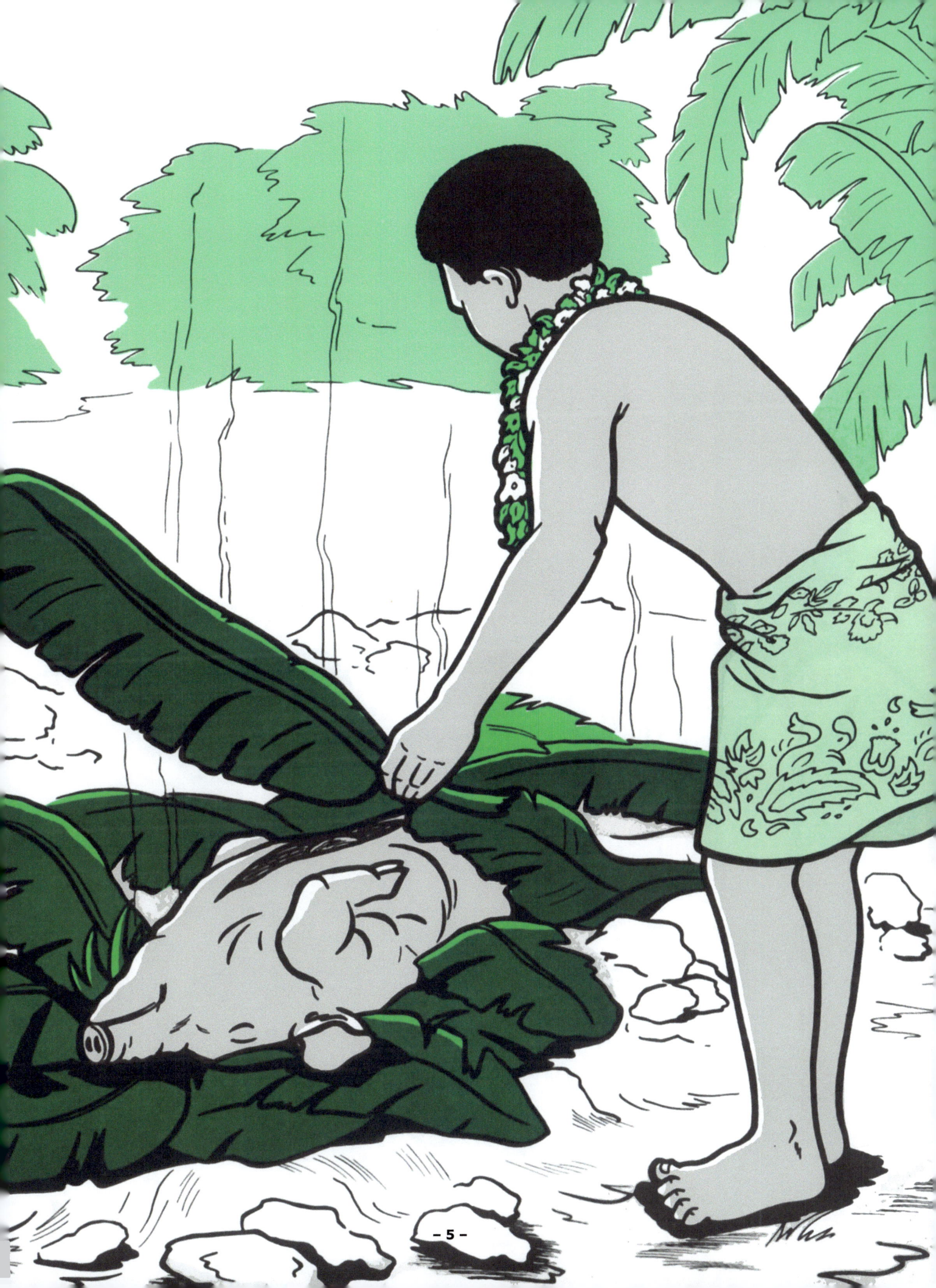

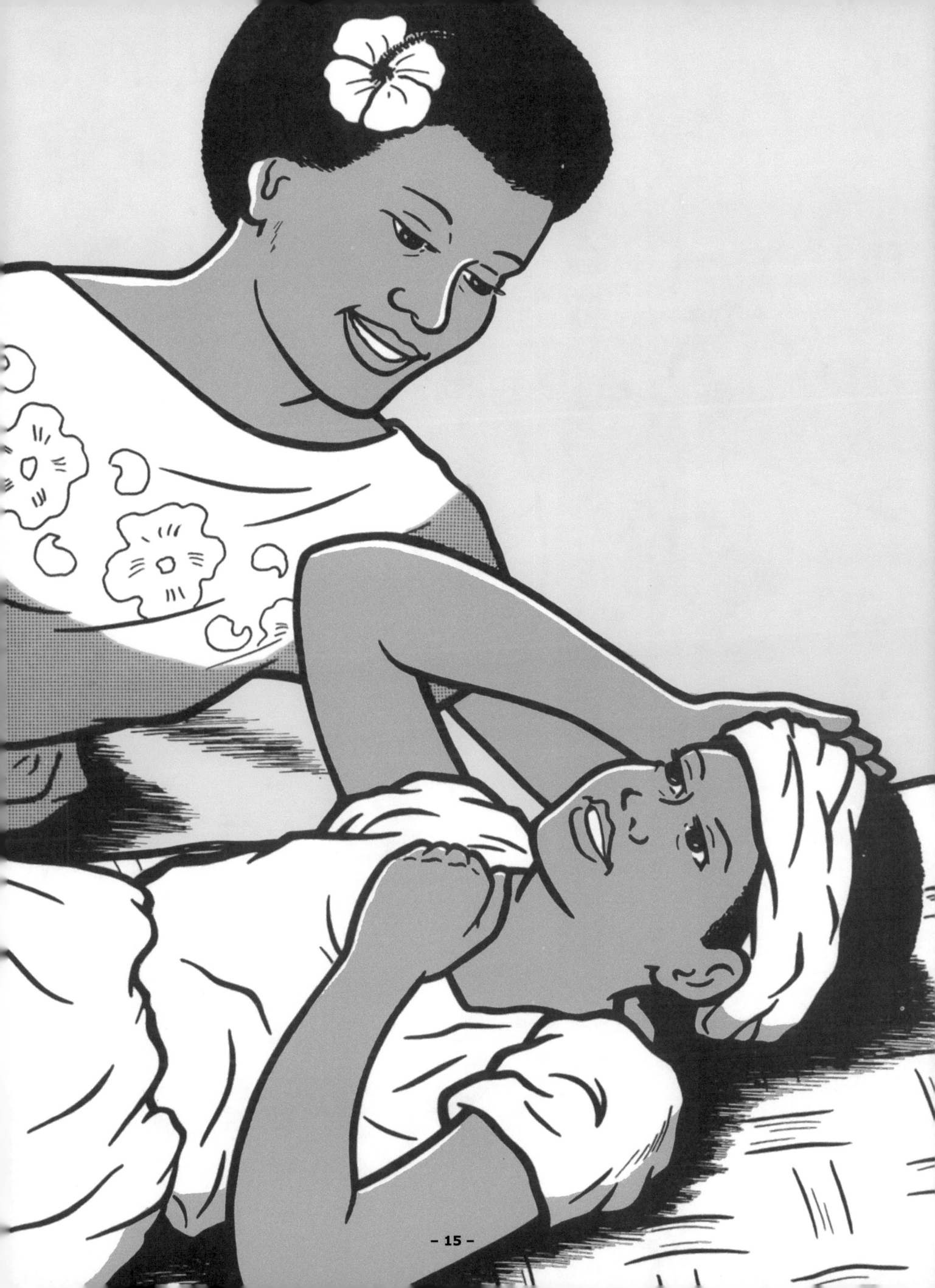

He that hath the Son hath life; and he that hath not the Son of God hath not life. These things have I written unto you that believe on the name of the Son of God; that ye may know that ye have eternal life, and that ye may believe on the name of the Son of God.

1 John 5:12-13

Chapter 1

Leba [pronounced *Lemba*] lay asleep on her sleeping mat in the corner of the vale [sometimes called a *bure*–a type of grass house] in which she lived with her mother and father on one of the islands of Fiji. One brown arm was across her eyes, as though to shut out the light. The tight, dark curls seemed to dance over her sleeping head.

Slowly her big brown eyes opened, as Leba felt her mother shaking her awake.

Show Illustration #1

Sitting up, Leba asked sleepily, "Where is Father?"

"You lazy girl!" her mother scolded. "Did you not hear the Tura ga-ni-Koro [Chief of the village] last night? This is the day of the big feast. Most of the men of the village have gone to catch fish for the feast. Your father is with them. And there is much work for us to do. Get up and eat your breakfast! You are the only girl in the village who is permitted to sleep this late."

"But I am only eight years old," Leba pouted.

"Eight years old! Many of the younger girls have been at work for a long time. Do not think because your name means *Princess* that you are one."

Leba remembered then. The night before, the chief had announced special orders for all the people in the village. Each one had been told what to do this day. Gladly they obeyed, for the people of these South Pacific islands loved their chief. They also loved the man who was governor of all the islands. He had been appointed by the queen of England. And they dearly loved and respected their queen.

Leba ate her breakfast of fish (which had been roasted on a hot stone), sticky dalo [a starchy vegetable], and some leftovers from the supper of the night before. There would be no more meals until the big feast which they would eat with neighbors. What a happy time they would have together! (Two meals a day were all that Leba had ever known.)

Each child of the village had been given extra work to do. Leba had to roll up the sleeping mats in her vale, sweep the mat which covered the floor made of earth and dry grass, and see that everything was clean and neat. After this she was free to play until her help was needed again. Leba was considered "spoiled" because she was an only child and her parents did not make her do as much work as other girls her age had to do.

Leba picked up her doll and went outside. She thought her doll was beautiful. It was made from the thick root of a plant, with a straight stick (forming arms) fastened to the root. The doll had two sticks for legs. Leba had heard about the dolls made of bottles, which the girls in the capital city (Suva) played with. But she was sure they could not be nicer than her own.

Leba walked down the path to where Bale lived, close to her vale. He had risen early to get his work done so he could be free to work on the little boat he was making.

Show Illustration #2

The sails were made of palm fronds but the boat itself was half a coconut shell.

"It's a nice boat, Bale," Leba said.

Bale only grunted. Leba thought he sounded a great deal like the pig which was his pet. The pig was nearby enjoying a nice, soft, muddy spot where the rain of the night had left a puddle.

Bale did not care about having girls around. But his good nature would not permit him to tell Leba to go home. So when Leba said, "Please, Bale, may I watch you sail your boat?" he grunted again.

Then he said, "Oh, all right. You may."

Down the path the two children hurried. When they reached the water they waded in up to their necks. Bale gave his boat a push and he and Leba watched as it sailed away in the bright sunlight. "It is a lovely boat, Bale," Leba said, watching the pleased expression on his face.

Girls like Leba are not so bad after all, Bale decided. They watched the boat until they could see it no longer.

Show Illustration #3

Then Leba and Bale sat on the beach and talked of the fun they would have that evening at the feast.

"And did you know, Bale, that my cousin Laniana is coming to the feast today? I'd better go home and see if she has arrived yet. She is going to stay with us for a few days."

"Well, I mean to keep out of her sight if I can," Bale said. "I don't like the things she says to me. You should not listen to her either, Leba. She is always trying to make us become the kind of Christian she is. Her talk about being 'saved from sin' and having 'salvation' is silly, I think."

"Yes, but I like the way she tells Bible stories. I don't have to believe them, Bale." Leba shrugged her shoulders and went off in search of another flower to put in her short, curly hair. Nothing bothered Leba for very long. She liked to dance and sing and play. Everything was wonderful to her as long as it pleased her. As she skipped along the path Leba stopped to watch some ladies weaving a long mat of palm leaves.

Show Illustration #4

Other women were pounding tree bark, making it into a cloth on which to spread the feast. Farther down the path a few more women were painting lovely designs on some of the cloth which had already been pounded and stretched. *Masi cloth*, they called it. [Sometimes it is called *tapa*.] Plaited coconut leaves were made ready to hold the pig, fish, vegetables, and other foods.

What a lot of work the women have to do! thought Leba. *I wish I could stay a little girl always. That is, if I could have my own parents, always. I don't like work, not one bit.*

But she would not think about it now. Work was not pleasant thinking for Leba, and she liked only pleasant things. Again she shrugged her shoulders and danced off, waving to Bale who was trudging along behind her. He had more work to do. And he did not like work either!

Chapter 2

Show Illustration #5

Pigs were roasting slowly in lovos [ovens in the earth]. Leba could see the smoke and steam rising above the lovos as she got closer to where the feast would be held. The delicious smell made her mouth water. Often she had seen men preparing the lovos. Logs were burned inside the holes in the earth, over which stones were heated to a white heat. On the hot stones were hard green plant stems. The whole pig was laid on the steaming hot stems and covered well with banana leaves and earth.

The white-hot stones reminded Leba of the firewalkers. She thought, *I wish I could walk on those stones and not get my feet burned. The firewalkers don't burn their feet. But I wonder how they do it! If no one were around, I'd try it myself, right this minute.*

Suddenly Leba felt warm arms around her shoulders. Turning, she exclaimed, "Oh, Laniana! You scared me! I didn't hear you coming. But I am glad–so very glad–you came to the feast. There is so much I want to know. You'll tell me more about the big city where you live, won't you? I love to hear about things which happen in Suva. Have they had a fire walking ceremony lately? I think it is wonderful that men can walk on those hot stones and not have their feet burned. Sometimes I feel like trying it myself when the men are preparing the lovos."

Laniana drew the little girl close to her. *Why is Laniana trembling?* Leba wondered. "Come, Leba, let's sit here in this shady spot away from the others, so we can talk."

"About the firewalkers, Laniana?"

"Yes, about the firewalkers."

Show Illustration #6

As they sat close together Laniana told Leba of the men who walked on hot, hot stones without burning their bare feet. She told how they stayed in a hut all of the night before without being disturbed. "They say they talk with a small devil, Leba."

Leba giggled. "I wonder what the devil says to them?"

"Leba, this is a serious thing. The men actually worship Satan. Satan has great power. Indeed, he is the one who keeps their feet from being burned. But, Leba, Satan is a deceiver. Someday these men will be truly sorry that they worshiped him. So will everyone who refuses to place their trust in the Lord Jesus as their Saviour from sin. Without Him, they cannot have salvation. (*Teacher:* Be sure your students understand the meaning of *Saviour*. Point out that the first part of *Saviour* reminds us of the word *save*. *Salvation* also includes the idea of being saved. The Lord Jesus died to *save* us from sin and its penalty–eternal death.)

Leba pouted. "Laniana, I don't want you to tell *me* again that I am a sinner and need salvation. *I am not a sinner!* I don't want to hear any more about this. I only want to hear happy things, Laniana. Please? Besides, I am a Christian. You know this. All Fijians are Christians."

A sad look came into the young woman's face. "But, Leba, I do not tell you these things to make you sad. It's only to make you happy–happier than you have ever been."

"But I'm not happy when you tell me about Jesus' being nailed to the cross and being made to die for me. I had nothing to do with it, Laniana. And I don't want to hear it again! Please, Laniana, tell me about the City of Suva where you live."

Show Illustration #7

Drawing the little girl into her arms, Laniana began. "In Suva, the big city (see map), there are Hindu temples–temples where the people from India pray to idols. The women wear beautiful saris. The sari is one long piece of cloth which they wrap around them gracefully. And I know you'd like to see the policemen. They wear long white gloves which come partway up their arms. Their white sulus [skirts] are all jagged around the bottom. The policemen are servants of our queen, you know."

"Is the queen very, very lovely, Laniana?" Leba asked.

"I have never seen her, Leba. But they say she is very lovely. Her skin is white. Instead of combing her hair upward, as we Fijians comb ours, she combs it downward. Her hair is soft. And, Leba," Laniana continued, "I feel our queen may have received the Lord Jesus as her Saviour."

Leba squirmed. "Tell me about the welcoming ceremony when they serve the yanggona."

Laniana sighed. "Well," she began, "an important visitor came to Suva just last week. The chief sat on the ground, with his men who sat silently in two lines facing each other. The guest of honor sat at the far end, facing the chief. The chief took ground root of the pepper plant and mixed it with cold water. Then he stirred and stirred. When he had finished, one of the men accepted some of the brownish mixture in a coconut shell cup.

Show Illustration #8

"The cup bearer held it with both hands and, walking stiff-legged, presented the yanggona to the visitor. This they did to let him know he was welcome."

"Did it make him drunk, Laniana?" Leba giggled.

"No, drinking it doesn't make anyone drunk. But it does make a person's tongue and mouth feel strange. For a time he has no feeling in his mouth. And if he drank a lot of it, his legs would seem to be paralyzed."

Right then the feast was announced. And Laniana, with a heavy heart, and Leba–as carefree as ever–hurried to enjoy it.

Chapter 3

The feast was over. Everything was neat and clean as everyone did carefully the tasks the village chief had assigned.

Show Illustration #9

Back in their vale Laniana sat with the family late into the night, talking. Leba, lying on her mat, *willed* to stay awake and listen. Away down in her heart she really wanted to know the meaning of the words *Saviour, saved* and *salvation* for her own life. *Laniana always speaks lovingly about the Lord Jesus*, Leba thought.

Laniana was saying, "A family from America has come to live in Suva."

"Why have they come?" Leba's father asked.

"They have come because they know and love the Lord Jesus."

"But what has this to do with their coming to our islands to live?" Leba's mother wanted to know.

"Well," Laniana answered, "they know that these islands were known long ago as the Cannibal Islands because the warriors killed and feasted on human beings. But after the Christians came, this changed."

"We still do not understand what this has to do with their choosing *our* islands as their home," Leba's father answered.

"Please do not be angry," Laniana said, "and please let me explain. These people are missionaries. They know it is not enough to believe *about* Jesus, to go to church and to call ourselves Christians because we do these things. In order truly to be a Christian, one must receive the Lord Jesus as his Saviour from sin [John 1:12]. God is holy. He cannot allow any man, woman or child to go to Heaven with sin in his heart. God will not allow sin in Heaven."

The group was quiet now. Laniana prayed (in her heart) that God would give her the right words to say–that she might make God's plan of salvation clear. She heard Leba squirm on her mat and knew the child was awake and listening.

"And yet," Laniana continued, "this God–the true and living God–loves all people everywhere. He wants them to live with Him in Heaven forever. And so He made a way."

Show Illustration #10

The happiness which was in Laniana's heart came through the tones of her voice and she said, "I have here some lovely pink shells." She held them up in the dim light. "Let's pretend you've done something wrong and the village chief has put you in prison. He says that you must pay a fine. And the fine is some nice pink shells. (Shells are sometimes used instead of money in the villages.) Then I come to visit you in prison. I give the shells to the chief and he lets you go free. I have *redeemed* you. I've paid the price to set you free."

"This," Laniana continued, "is what the missionaries have come to tell us. They know we Fijians often call ourselves Christians. But we really are not Christians any more than the Indians from India who live on our islands and worship idols. We're not Christians unless we believe in our hearts that Jesus is the Son of God and place our trust in Him as our Saviour from sin. Then we become true children of God and receive His gift of salvation."

Laniana knew that Leba's parents did not like what she was saying. But she continued eagerly. "Suppose when I came to redeem you from prison, and gave my shells to the chief, you would say, 'No! I do not *want* to leave the prison! Let the chief keep the shells. *I* will not allow Laniana to pay for my sins.' Then you *could not* be set free because you *would not*."

Leba giggled to herself as she listened. *That would be a silly thing to do*, she thought.

Show Illustration #11

Laniana continued, "Don't you see? Jesus, God's Son, redeemed us by dying on the cross for us. We will never have to take the punishment of death for our sins if our trust is in Him. He paid the penalty for us."

Leba turned over on her mat, yawning sleepily. She had done nothing wrong. She was not going to be put in prison. She didn't need *anyone* to pay for her! Yet, somehow, she could not sleep.

Show Illustration #12

Leba kept thinking about those lovely pink shells. How she would like to have just one!

Leba pretended to be asleep when Laniana lay down on the mat next to her. But from under her eyelashes, she peeked to see where Laniana placed those lovely shells.

And so, a little girl who refused the Lord Jesus because she thought she was not a sinner, planned how she could steal from her cousin.

Laniana was soon asleep. Not so Leba. All sleepiness seemed to be gone from her now. She was wide awake. Slowly–carefully–she rolled toward the shells. Quietly she chose the prettiest one and silently hid it under her mat.

Chapter 4

The next week Laniana was back again visiting in the village. She had come to take part in the balolo [tiny sea worms] festival. Leba was nervous. She hoped Laniana had not missed the shell. But as they sat together Laniana said, "When I got home, after my visit here last week, my loveliest pink shell was missing. I think I may have dropped it when I was showing them to your mother and father. Did you find one, Leba, when you swept the mat?"

Show Illustration #13

"No! No! I did not see any–*not any at all*." Laniana gave the girl a strange look but said nothing more.

Leba shrugged her shoulders and began talking excitedly about the balolo she hoped to catch. Then she hurried off with the others to the sea. (Leba had coaxed her father into letting her go, even though children did not usually do this.)

They would camp on the beach all night in order to be ready when the sea worms rose to the surface. According to the moon and the sun this was the time the balolo would leave the coral ridges and come to shore.

Leba's father was one of the few who went out in a canoe very early the next morning. Leba was not supposed to go in the canoe with her father. But as he pushed away from the shore the willful girl jumped in.

Soon the water was covered with wriggling balolo. Up they came! Blue, red, yellow, purple, green, white, brown. Everyone tried to scoop up as many as they could with a bucket or a net.

What a happy time the villagers had! They laughed and shouted as they tried to catch the balolo quickly, before the hungry fish got them. It was a contest between the villagers and the fish. How much fun it was! The balolo would make a delicious meal for whoever caught them–fish or man.

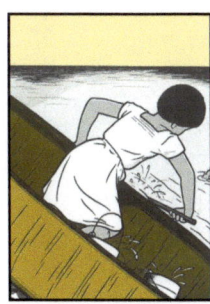

Show Illustration #14

Leba was so excited she kept leaning way out, trying to catch more and still more in her net. Her father shouted, "Watch out, Leba! Don't lean out so far! You'll upset the canoe!"

Carefree little Leba paid no attention to her father's warning. Her net was full of the wriggling sea worms. Holding her net high with one hand, Leba used her other hand to scare away a fish.

"Watch out!" her father shouted. But it was too late. Over went the canoe and into the water went Leba and her father, sea worms slithering all over them.

Leba's father grumbled, "That silly, spoiled girl. Why did I allow her to come with me? Other girls stay home where they belong. But where is she? I don't see her anywhere."

Smoothly, and as quickly as the fish went after the balolo, Leba's father dove among the coral rocks. There he found Leba, blood oozing from her head. She had struck a rock as the canoe overturned.

Neighbors helped Leba's father pull the unconscious girl into their canoe and raced for the shore. The villagers helped carry Leba back to the vale and placed her on a sleeping mat.

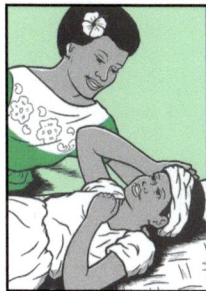

Show Illustration #15

Together, Leba's mother and Laniana bound the wound in Leba's head. The little girl opened her eyes. "What happened?" she asked weakly, putting her hand to her bandaged head.

It was not the hurt in Leba's head which made her look sad. It was the hurt in her heart. Slowly she reached out and took Laniana's hand.

"Laniana, I am sorry–I stole your pink shell," she said.

Laniana's eyes filled with tears. "I forgive you," she said quickly. Then she added, "But, Leba, if you had been conscious when your father came to lift you out of the water, would you have pushed him away? Would you have said, 'Leave me alone! I do not need to be saved'?"

The corners of Leba's mouth turned up. "Of course not," she said. "I am not that foolish!"

Laniana sat quietly looking at the little girl for a moment. "But, Leba, this is exactly what you are doing to the Lord Jesus. He wants to save you and take you to Heaven someday. And you say you do not need Him. But you *know* you do. It is sin in your heart which made you steal the shell. It is sin which made you tell a lie about it when I asked if you had seen it."

Leba's face was serious as she said, "But *how* can He save me, Laniana–how can He?"

Carefully then, and gently, Laniana explained to Leba that the Lord Jesus is the Son of God.

Show Illustration #16

"Believe He took the punishment of death for your sins, Leba. If there could have been any other way for us to get to Heaven, God would not have caused His dear Son to die such an awful death." Over and over she repeated, "'For God so loved the world, that He gave His only begotten Son, that whosoever believeth in Him should not perish but have everlasting life'" (John 3:16).

Then she added, "Leba, let us say it this way. You repeat after me, 'For God so loved *Leba*, that He gave His only begotten Son, that *Leba*, who believeth in Him should not perish, but have everlasting life.'"

Leba–with eyes closed–repeated the words after Laniana. Then a beautiful smile came over her face. She opened her eyes. "I do believe, Laniana! I believe with all my heart! I do! I do!"

Chapter 5

Leba's mother had been sitting in a corner of the vale as Laniana talked to Leba. When she saw the beautiful smile on her child's face she thought, *What Laniana said must be true!*

When Leba began to nap, her mother talked for a long time with Laniana about knowing God, and having forgiveness of sin by trusting in the Lord Jesus Christ who died on the cross. "Laniana," she said, "when you talked last week about paying a ransom for someone who was in prison for wrong-doing, I began to understand a little. *But I did not want to believe.* I thought we were Christians. Today, I do want to believe. Tell me how, Laniana, please."

Gladly Laniana explained over and over again, that God loves *all* people everywhere and has provided a pardon for each one who will receive it.

Show Illustration #17

All this time Bale had been outside, waiting for word of his playmate. Yet when Laniana came to the door and said, "She is all right, Bale, and will be as good as new," he just grunted. *Silly girl,* he thought. *Her father ought to punish her. He should have known better than to allow a girl to try to catch balolo.*

Show Illustration #18

The next day was Sunday. Leba could only lie quietly on her sleeping mat. But she listened happily to the sound of the lali calling the people to church. (The lali–pronounced *lolli*, as in lollipop–is made of a hollowed tree trunk and is pounded as a drum.)

Leba knew the worshipers would begin their service by singing questions and answers–all on one note. *Chanting,* they called it. The questions and answers were all about God and the Bible. Leba loved to hear these chants, especially when they told familiar Bible events.

Leba spoke to her mother, sitting close by. "Mother, next week or whenever my head is better and we go to church–I shall understand better the chants, now that I have received the Lord Jesus as my very own Saviour."

"And so shall I, my child, for you see, Leba, I too have believed in my heart and have become a true Christian."

Leba raised up on her elbow. "And Father, too? Has Father become a Christian?"

"I do not think your father has become a Christian–not yet, at least, Leba. But I am sure he will very soon. You know how much he loves you. Perhaps if you ask him to receive the Lord Jesus as his Saviour he will do it. I am sure he understands now that there is a difference in *saying* we are Christians and really being saved.

"You have always been a smiling child, Leba. But the smile on your face now is more beautiful than the loveliest sunset. I am sure your father has noticed. And he knows what has put it there."

That very night Leba's father talked for hours with Laniana. Finally, fully convinced, he too received the Lord Jesus as his Saviour and Lord.

Leba wanted to jump up and down when she learned about her father's decision. "Bale, my playmate, is next," she said. "I am sure he will listen to me. Tell me again, Laniana, just what to say to him. Tomorrow I am going after Bale!"

Show Illustration #19

Exactly as she had planned, the very next day Leba walked down the path, head still wrapped in bandages, to Bale who was working on another boat. Bale was pleased to see her.

"Bale, I have come to talk to you, if you will listen to a silly girl."

Bale grunted.

"Now, please, Bale, will you stop grunting like your pet pig and listen to me for a few moments? You know I might not have been here if Father had not been quick to get me out of the ocean. So will you please listen to me for a few minutes? You do not need to talk, but, *please* do stop grunting."

Bale laughed. Quick to take advantage of his good humor, Leba began telling him how she, her mother and father had become true Christian believers. She forgot many of the things Laniana had told her. It did not matter, for when Bale saw the tears running down the cheeks of his carefree playmate, he was amazed. And listen he did!

Finally Bale spoke. "I do not understand all of this at all, Leba. And I can't do something just to please you–nothing as important as this. But I am willing to listen and try to understand. Do you suppose Laniana would explain these things to me?"

Laniana had been watching from the door of the vale. When Leba motioned to her, she hurried down the path. "He is ready," Leba said, again smiling her lovely smile. "Tell him, Laniana, tell him."

Show Illustration #20

As Leba started back toward the vale, she laid her weak hand on Laniana's arm, saying, "Do you know something, Laniana? If it hadn't been for those sea worms I might still be without salvation. It's really wonderful to have the Lord Jesus in my heart and *know* I have everlasting life!"